9755
PAR

Parker, Janice
Wyoming

34880000823563

WYOMING

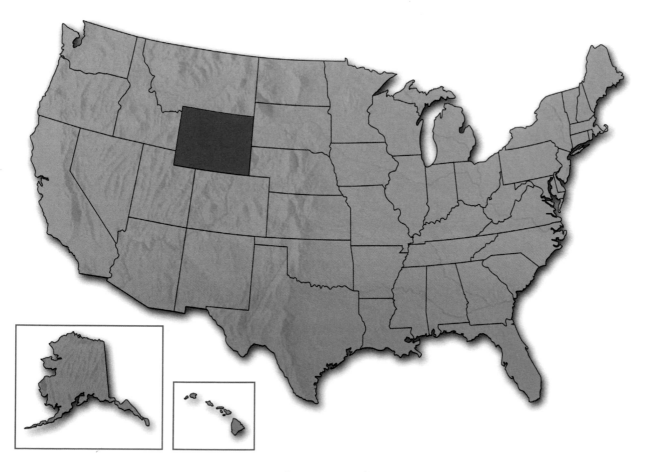

Janice Parker

Published by Weigl Publishers Inc.
123 South Broad Street, Box 227
Mankato, MN   56002
USA
Web site: http://www.weigl.com

Library of Congress Cataloging-in-Publication Data

Parker, Janice.
    Wyoming / Janice Parker.
         p. cm. -- (A kid's guide to American states)
    ISBN 1-930954-63-8
     1. Wyoming--Juvenile literature. [1. Wyoming.] I. Title. II. Series.

F761.3 .P37 2001

2001017996

ISBN 1-930954-07-7 (pbk.)

Printed in the United States of America
1 2 3 4 5 6 7 8 9 10   05 04 03 02 01

Project Coordinator
Michael Lowry
Substantive Editor
Rennay Craats
Copy Editor
Bryan Pezzi
Designers
Warren Clark
Terry Paulhus
Layout
Susan Kenyon
Photo Researcher
Diana Marshall

Photograph Credits

Every reasonable effort has been made to trace ownership and to obtain
permission to reprint copyright material. The publishers would be
pleased to have any errors or omissions brought to their attention so
that they may be corrected in subsequent printings.

Cover: little cowboy (Randy Wells), jeans pattern (Hemera Studios); **Jim Baron/The Image Finders:** page 14B; **Eric R. Berndt/The Image Finders:** page 9T; **Cheyenne Area Convention & Visitors Bureau:** pages 14T, 20BL, 21T, 28BL; **Corbis Corporation:** pages 9BR, 13B; **Corel Corporation:** pages 4BL, 5BL, 27BR; **Digital Vision Ltd.:** page 20T, **EyeWire, Inc.:** pages 13T, 15BL; **Jackson Hole Chamber of Commerce:** pages 7T, 24BL, 25B; **Adam Jahiel/City of Sheridan Convention & Visitors Bureau:** page 22BL; **Michael S. Miller Photography:** pages 6T, 26T; **Steve Mulligan Photography:** pages 8T, 10T; **Park County Travel Council:** pages 22T, 24T; **Photo by Ray E. Harris/Wyoming State Geological Survey:** page 9BL; **PhotoDisc, Inc.:** page 28TL; © **Pollock-Krasner Foundation/ARS (New-York)/SODRAC (Montreal) 2000 (©Archivo Iconografico, S.A./CORBIS):** page 25T; **Reproduced under the permission of the State of Wyoming:** page 7BL; **Al Townschend/IPSSSDR:** page 27BL; **Andrea Wells:** pages 12T, 12BL; **Randy Wells:** pages 3B, 5T, 6BL, 7BR, 11B, 15BR, 21B, 24BR, 27T, 29TR; © **Wyoming's Wind River Country:** pages 20BR, 23B, 26B; **Marilyn "Angel" Wynn:** page 16BR; **University of Wyoming Photo Service:** page 15T; **Wyoming Division of Cultural Resources/State Archives:** pages 16T, 16BL, 17T, 17BL, 17BR, 18T, 18B, 19T, 19BL, 19BR; **The Wyoming Division of Tourism:** pages 3T (Grand Teton Lodge Co.), 3M, 4T (Randy Wagner), 4BR (Holger Leue), 6BR, 8B, 10BL, 10BR, 11T (Grand Teton Lodge Co.), 12BR, 22BR, 23T (Cassandra Shrikhande), 29BL.

CONTENTS

INTRODUCTION

"Nature had collected all of her beauties together in one chosen place." That was explorer John C. Fremont's description of Wyoming when he first set eyes on the state in 1842. Since then, many others have admired Wyoming's breathtaking natural beauty. As a result of this inspiring landscape, the state enjoys a special place in the country's history. Wyoming is home to the first land to be set aside as a nationally protected area—Yellowstone National Park. While many other remarkable natural regions are associated with Wyoming, such as Grand Teton National Park, Jackson Hole, and Devil's Tower, no other national park can equal Yellowstone's historic appeal.

Wagon trains are a great way to explore Wyoming's open plains. On four-day long trips adventurers camp under the stars and listen to cowboy ballads around the campfire.

QUICK FACTS

The state flag has a white buffalo with the state seal on its side. The buffalo stands against a blue background. The flag's white border is a symbol of purity, while the red represents the state's Native-American population.

Yellowstone National Park became the world's first national park in 1872.

The state mammal is the bison, the state bird is the meadowlark, and the state reptile is the horned toad.

The 1,267-foot Devil's Tower is a sacred site of worship for many Native Americans. Legend tells of a giant bear who once sharpened its claws on the rock.

Travelers of Wyoming's highways are treated to majestic views of the state's scenic landscape.

Getting There

Wyoming is located in the western United States. It is bordered by Montana to the north and west, South Dakota and Nebraska to the east, Colorado to the south, Utah to the south and east, and Idaho to the west.

Getting around in Wyoming is easy. Three major state highways cross Wyoming. Wyoming has about 28,456 miles of highway, including more than 900 miles of federal interstate highway. Wyoming is also accessible to travelers by air. There are 142 airports in the state, many of which are private airstrips. Wyoming's major cities all have airports, although they are not busy by national standards.

QUICK FACTS

The state seal shows a woman in front of an equal rights banner. A cowboy on the left side represents the ranching industry, while a miner on the right side represents the mining industry. The seal was adopted in 1893.

Wyoming has 1,976 miles of railroad. Goods, such as coal, are often shipped by rail.

Wyoming Location Map

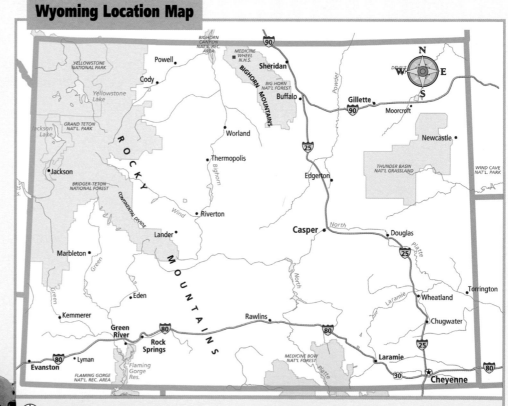

⭐ **Capital:** Cheyenne

🛡 **Interstate highways**

Scale 0 10 20 Mi. / 0 10 20 30 Km.

Population: 493,700

Size: 97,818 square miles

Highest peak: Gannett Peak 13,804 ft.

A small herd of bison spends the summer in Grand Teton National Park. Each year, more than 4 million people visit the park.

During Wyoming's early days, the state was an essential corridor to the West. Most of the historic trails to the West cut through Wyoming. The Oregon, California, and Mormon Trails lead through the South Pass of the Continental Divide, in southwestern Wyoming. The Continental Divide follows a ridge of mountains that runs from Alaska, through Canada, and then down the western United States through Wyoming, and on to Mexico. The **terrain** was a challenge for the thousands of early pioneers who traveled through the region. For those who settled in Wyoming, a lack of good cropland made it difficult for them to earn a living.

Today, Wyoming is one of the country's most attractive recreational states. Lakes and rivers are used for boating and fishing. Forests, full of plant and animal life, attract hunters and wildlife observers. The mountains and the national parks are popular destinations for campers, hikers, and backpackers.

Wagon ruts from the historic Oregon Trail can still be seen in Wyoming. The more than 2,000-mile-long trail once took pioneers from Missouri to Oregon.

CONTINENTAL DIVIDE ELEVATION 8262

The slopes at Jackson Hole are the perfect place for cowboys to relax during Wyoming's winter months.

Known as "The Equality State," Wyoming was the first state to give equal rights and opportunities to women. It was the first state to allow women to vote and to hold public office, and the first to allow women to serve on juries. Wyoming also had the country's first female judge, the first female state legislator, and the first female governor.

Wyoming is also known as "The Cowboy State." This nickname pays tribute to the hard work and independence of early ranchers and pioneers. Cattle drives, rodeos, roundups, and dude ranches are all part of Wyoming's charm and culture. Wyoming is the real "Wild West," whose history has inspired countless songs, movies, and stories.

QUICK FACTS

The state of Wyoming has a registered trademark—the Bucking Horse and Rider. People across the country associate the image with Wyoming. The trademark was copyrighted in 1936.

Connecticut, Delaware, Hawaii, Maryland, Massachusetts, New Hampshire, New Jersey, Rhode Island, Vermont, and West Virginia could all fit within Wyoming's borders at the same time.

Frontier Days in Cheyenne is a celebration of Wyoming's cowboy culture. Rodeo events, concerts, and carnival rides are all a part of this yearly ten-day festival in July.

Ayers Natural Bridge in Wyoming is one of the few natural bridges in the world to have water flowing under it.

QUICK FACTS

The highest point in Wyoming is Gannett Peak, at 13,804 feet above sea level.

Wyoming is the windiest state in the nation, with wind speeds averaging 13 miles per hour.

Wyoming's average precipitation is 13 inches per year.

LAND AND CLIMATE

Wyoming is the ninth-largest state in the nation. The eastern third of the state is made up of the Great Plains. The region's flat prairies and short grasses make it excellent for raising cattle and sheep. A large portion of the state is covered by the Rocky Mountain System. In this region, deep valleys and wide basins separate the mountain ranges.

The Continental Divide stretches from the southcentral area of the state up through the northwest. The Divide's mountainous terrain supports shrubs and bushes, but not trees.

Wyoming's climate is cool, dry, and sunny. Average July temperatures range from 63° Fahrenheit in the mountainous northwest to 68°F in the southeast. In winter, January temperatures drop to 19°F in the northwest and 27°F in the southeast. The greatest amount of rain and snow falls in the mountains, while the plains and basins receive little **precipitation**.

The Rocky Mountains cover the western and central portion of Wyoming.

NATURAL RESOURCES

About one-fifth of Wyoming is covered in forests. Trees such as pine, spruce, and fir provide a valuable natural resource. Most of the state's forests grow in the mountain regions where rainfall is highest. Wyoming's lumber industry logs Douglas firs, ponderosa pines, and lodgepole pines.

Wyoming is rich in mineral resources. Wyoming has the largest reserve of the mineral trona on Earth. The reserve is estimated at 50 to 100 billion tons. Large deposits of bentonite are also found in the state. Bentonite is used as an ingredient in glue, cosmetics, toothpaste, and paint. Other natural resources found in Wyoming include coal, natural gas, feldspar, agate, jade, limestone, gravel, and gypsum. The most valuable resource in the state is natural gas. The state produces about 760 billion cubic feet of natural gas per year.

Trees logged in Wyoming are used to make plywood, pulp, and other paper products.

QUICK FACTS

Wyoming has been called the "Trona Capital of the World." The state produces about 17 million tons of trona per year. Wyoming's trona industry employs nearly 3,000 people.

Wyoming has eight of the largest coal deposits in the country.

Wyoming ranks first among the states in the production of gemstones. Jade, moss agate, ruby, jasper, bloodstone, and star sapphire have all been found in the state.

Coal can be found underneath one-half of Wyoming. The coal is normally transported out of the state by train.

Jade

The lodgepole pine grows well in the higher mountains of Wyoming, where the climate is cool and wet.

PLANTS AND ANIMALS

Wyoming is home to a wide variety of plants and animals. In the mountains, lodgepole pine and Douglas fir trees are plentiful. Mosses, lichens, and wildflowers, such as Indian paintbrush and forget-me-nots, cover the state. At lower elevations, aspens, cottonwoods, and willows grow. The lowlands are home to many species of sagebrush. In the west, sagebrushes form **scrubland**. Western wheatgrass, junegrass, and fringed sagewort are other sagebrush species that grow in Wyoming. The Great Plains region has more than 150 different types of grasses, such as bluegrass. The driest regions of the state are home to plants that require little water to grow, such as yuccas and cactuses.

QUICK FACTS

Wyoming is home to about 2,200 different types of plants.

Wyoming has four national wildlife preserves, nine national forests, and two national parks.

The state tree of Wyoming is the cottonwood. It can be found along riverbanks throughout the state.

The Indian paintbrush is Wyoming's state flower. It is also known as the painted cup.

Just over 1,300 bison can be found in Yellowstone National Park.

Wyoming has more pronghorn antelopes than anywhere else in North America. The state also has the largest elk herd in the world. Mule deer are found throughout the state, while white-tailed deer live in the Black Hills area. The northwestern part of the state is home to moose, and herds of bison are found in Yellowstone and Grand Teton National Parks. Bighorn sheep live in the northern part of the state. Wyoming also has rabbits, coyotes, and bobcats living within its borders.

Many birds make their home in Wyoming. The sage grouse lives throughout the state. Other Wyoming birds include pheasants, partridges, wild turkeys, ducks, and geese. White pelicans, trumpeter swans, and whistler swans can also be found in the state. Wyoming has bass, walleye, perch, channel catfish, trout, and many other species of fish swimming in its streams and lakes.

QUICK FACTS

Black bears can be found throughout much of Wyoming's forested regions. Grizzly bears live in the higher mountain and wilderness areas in and around Yellowstone Park.

Thousands of elk spend their winter at the National Elk Refuge. *Wapiti*, a Shawnee word meaning "white rump," is another name for elk.

Pronghorn antelopes can run at speeds of more than 60 miles per hour.

The Old Faithful geyser expels between 3,700 and 8,400 gallons of boiling water per eruption.

TOURISM

Yellowstone National Park is the state's most popular tourist destination. The park is known for its geysers, which are fountains of hot water and steam that erupt from the earth. The water is forced out from superheated underground mineral springs. The most well-known geyser is Old Faithful, whose blasts last for 5 minutes and can reach more than 180 feet in height.

Grand Teton National Park rivals Yellowstone as the most picturesque park in Wyoming. The park is home to about 200 miles of trails and many of its mountain peaks rise more than 12,000 feet above sea level.

Visitors to the Wyoming Dinosaur Center in Thermopolis can tour the museum or participate in an archeological dig. The museum has nineteen full-size dinosaur skeletons, including an allosaur, a triceratops, and a tyrannosaurus rex. While in Thermopolis, tourists can visit the mineral pools to bathe in the world's largest natural hot springs.

Located in the northwest corner of Wyoming, Grand Teton National Park features some of the youngest mountains in the Rocky Mountain System.

INDUSTRY

Mining is Wyoming's most important industry. More than 18,000 Wyomingites work in mining. More coal is produced in Wyoming than in any other state. A portion of the state's coal is burned to create electricity. Wyoming's coal is also used to generate electricity in twenty-two other states. The state also produces a large amount of **hydroelectricity**, most of which is exported to other states.

Wyoming is the fifth largest producer of natural gas and the sixth largest producer of oil in the country. The state produces about 1.2 trillion cubic feet of natural gas per year. Wyoming produces as much as 65 million barrels of oil per year.

Manufacturing plants in Wyoming process the raw materials mined in the state, including coal, iron ore, copper, petroleum, and sodium carbonate. Wyoming's chemical plants produce fertilizers and other agricultural chemicals.

There are more than 17,000 oil and gas wells in Wyoming.

QUICK FACTS

About 98 percent of the state's electricity comes from the burning of coal.

Wyoming produces about 335 million tons of coal per year.

Sodium carbonate is used in glass, baking soda, and paper.

The majority of Wyoming's hydroelectric plants are located on the North Platte River.

Wyoming is home to some 9,200 farms and ranches. More than half of these farms rely on irrigation to grow crops.

GOODS AND SERVICES

Almost all of the agricultural land in Wyoming is used for ranching. Beef cattle and sheep are important to the state's economy. The sheep are raised mainly for wool, while the sale of beef cattle accounts for two-thirds of the state's farm income. Wyoming has very few farms, since there is not enough precipitation for most crops to grow well. A few farms in the eastern part of the state grow beans, potatoes, corn, grains, and sugar beets. Other important crops include alfalfa, barley, wheat, and hay.

Various types of machinery, such as construction and farm equipment, are produced in Wyoming factories. Food-processing plants produce beet sugar, flour, and cheese. Wyoming also manufactures clothing, cement, and glass.

QUICK FACTS

Over half of the state of Wyoming, 30 million acres, is owned by the government.

Wyoming's ranches contain close to 824,000 beef cows, and 660,000 sheep and lambs.

Wyoming ranks second in the nation in wool production.

Wool production in Wyoming has been valued at $6.2 million per year.

About one-quarter of Wyoming's workers are employed in the service industry. This includes jobs such as restaurant workers, lawyers, and medical workers. A large majority of people in Wyoming work for the government. Many of these people work in the national forests and parks. The Francis E. Warren Air Force Base near Cheyenne employs about 3,600 military personnel. The base began as a cavalry post for the United States Army in 1867. Today, the base serves as the home of Air Force Space Command's 90th Space Wing.

Wyoming's small population means that few towns can support medical centers. Many towns in the state are without doctors and hospitals. Patients often travel great distances to receive medical care.

Education is a priority in Wyoming. For children between the ages of 7 and 16, attendance at school is **compulsory**. Wyoming spends more money on education than any other state except Alaska.

More than 11,000 students attend the University of Wyoming, which occupies 785 acres of land.

QUICK FACTS

The University of Wyoming opened in 1887 in Laramie when Wyoming was still a territory.

More than 262,000 people are employed in Wyoming.

The first newspaper in Wyoming, the *Daily Telegraph*, began in Fort Bridger in 1863.

More than 35 percent of Wyomingites have access to the Internet.

Park Rangers at Yellowstone National Park provide visitors with information on the different types of wildlife found within the park.

FIRST NATIONS

With the arrival of the horse, many Shoshones began living as ranchers and farmers.

Archeologists have found evidence of people living in Wyoming as far back as 11,000 years ago. These early residents lived in caves and hunted big game, such as **mammoths** and bison. Some of these groups left behind pictures that were carved and painted onto rocks.

Over time, many First Nations groups came to settle in Wyoming. One of the largest was the Shoshones who lived in the Green River Valley. Another group, the Arapahos, lived south of the North Platte River. The Crows, the Cheyennes, the Lakotas, the Blackfoot, the Northern Utes, and the Bannocks also lived in Wyoming.

The lives of Native Americans in the Wyoming area changed drastically with the arrival of horses and guns. The Spanish brought the first horses to the area around 1680. Horses allowed Native Americans to travel much faster and over greater distances. In the mid-1700s, Native Peoples traded for guns with British and French settlers on the eastern coast of North America. These weapons enabled Native Peoples to hunt more efficiently.

Beadwork became part of the Shoshone culture when European explorers and traders offered beads in exchange for furs, skins, pemmican and other items.

The Green River Rendezvous was once an important meeting spot for Wyoming's trappers and traders.

EXPLORERS AND MISSIONARIES

The first European to explore Wyoming was John Colter. He was part of the Lewis and Clark expedition. Colter left the expedition in 1806 to become a trapper and trader. The following year he reached what is now Yellowstone National Park. A few years later, Colter returned to the east with stories of the large number of fur-covered animals in the area.

During the 1820s, hundreds of men traveled to Wyoming to work as trappers and to trade with the Native Peoples. These men, called "mountain men," gathered each year at a **rendezvous**. They traded with Native Americans, held great feasts, played games, sang songs, and danced. Eventually, forts were built and they became meeting places. Early rendezvous only lasted a couple of days, while later ones lasted more than two months. The last rendezvous was held in 1840, when the beavers in the region had almost disappeared. The beavers were the main source of fur for the mountain men, and as a result they were over trapped.

Mountain men often had interesting names such as Jeremiah "Liver Eatin'" Johnston and Thomas "Broken Hand" Fitzpatrick.

Wyoming's first oil well was established in Fremont County at Dallas Dome.

EARLY SETTLERS

Many settlers traveled through Wyoming on the Oregon Trail. Fort Laramie was an important stop for them. It was the last place to purchase supplies before entering the mountains. Once through the mountains, the settlers reached Independence Rock, where they carved their names into the stone. This was their way of letting friends and family who followed know that they had made it through the mountains safely.

Some of those who passed through Wyoming decided to settle in the area. Early pioneers had many conflicts with the local Native Peoples. The settlers often killed or drove away animals that the Native Peoples depended on for food. There were many battles over the years, and both sides suffered losses. In 1868, Native Americans in Wyoming signed peace **treaties** with the United States government. According to the treaties, Native Peoples would allow roads and railroads to be built in exchange for land.

Q UICK F ACTS

The first oil well in Wyoming was drilled in 1883.

The Oregon Trail was also used by **Mormons** to reach Salt Lake City, Utah, where they built a religious community. The section where the trail breaks off for Utah is called the Mormon Trail.

One out of every ten travelers died on the Oregon Trail, usually from **cholera**, poor living conditions, or accidental gunshots.

The California Trail was formed when a party led by John Bidwell broke off from the Oregon Trail and headed toward California.

Independence Rock was nicknamed the "Great Register of the Desert," because more than 5,000 names have been carved onto its surface.

By 1903, one out of every ten workers in Wyoming worked as a miner.

QUICK FACTS

During the cold winter of 1886–1887, hundreds of thousands of cattle died because they could not find food or water in the deep snow.

In 1920, the town of Jackson elected an all-women government.

In 1902, Shoshone became the first national forest in the United States. Devil's Tower became the first national monument in 1906.

In 1867, gold was discovered in the South Pass, attracting thousands of miners to the region. That same year, the Union Pacific Railroad came to Wyoming. Cities sprang up along the railroad line, including Cheyenne in 1867, and Laramie in 1868. Some people came to work on the railroad. Others arrived to purchase cheap land or open businesses. When Wyoming became a territory in 1868, more than 11,000 people had settled in the area.

Wyoming's land was well suited to cattle ranching. Soon, the region was covered in ranches, and many people came from the east to work as cowboys or to start their own ranches. By the mid-1880s, cattle ranching in Wyoming was at an all-time high. More than 1 million cattle could be found grazing on the plains. Disaster struck in 1886, when a severe **drought**, a harsh winter, and low prices forced many ranchers out of business.

Ranching in Wyoming began when large herds of cattle were driven to the state from Texas.

Nine out of ten Wyomingites over the age of 25 have a high school diploma.

Cheyenne

POPULATION

Wyoming has the smallest population out of all the fifty states. Today, about 493,700 people call the Cowboy State home. Cheyenne is the largest city, with a population of 53,600. Casper follows closely behind, with a population of 48,500. The next four largest cities are Laramie, Rock Springs, Gillette, and Sheridan. Cities and towns play an important role in Wyoming. With so few people and so much land, towns are a place for people to meet and stay in touch with their distant neighbors. Wyoming has a **population density** of about 5 people per square mile. The national average is 77 people per square mile.

There are about 11,000 Native Americans in Wyoming. About half live on the Wind River Reservation in western Wyoming. More than half of the Native Americans in Wyoming are either Arapahos or Shoshones. About 2,357 Shoshones and 3,501 Arapahos live on the Wind River Reservation.

The Wind River Reservation is the only Native-American reservation in Wyoming.

The Governor's Mansion, in Cheyenne, was once home to Nellie Tayloe Ross, the first woman governor in the country.

POLITICS AND GOVERNMENT

Wyoming's government is divided into three branches—the legislative, the executive, and the judicial. The legislative branch creates laws for the state and consists of a House of Representatives and a Senate. There are thirty state senators elected to four-year terms, and sixty-four representatives elected to two-year terms. The executive branch of government enforces state laws. It consists of the governor, auditor, treasurer, superintendent of public instruction, and secretary of state. All members are elected to four-year terms. The judicial branch is made up of the state's courts. The Supreme Court is the state's highest court.

Wyoming is divided into twenty-three counties. Each county is governed by a board of commissioners, who are elected to four-year terms. All the **municipalities** are run by a mayor and a city council, except Casper and Laramie, which are run by a city manager and a city council.

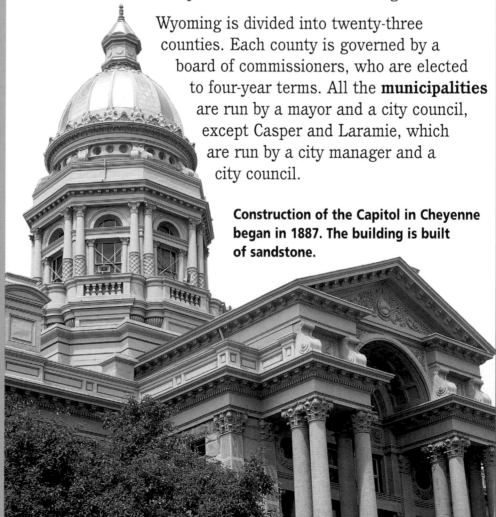

Construction of the Capitol in Cheyenne began in 1887. The building is built of sandstone.

QUICK FACTS

Wyoming's constitution was adopted in 1889.

In 1924, Nellie Tayloe Ross became the first woman in the country to be elected governor of a state. Ross served as Wyoming's governor until 1926.

During the 1924 election Nellie Tayloe Ross refused to campaign. She claimed "my candidacy is in the hands of my friends." Ross defeated her rival by 8,000 votes.

Wyoming is represented in the federal government by two senators and one member of the House of Representatives. Wyoming has three electoral votes in presidential elections.

Cheyenne's historic Governor's Mansion was home to Wyoming's governors from 1904 until 1976.

The Old Trail Town is made up of twenty-six historic buildings. Some of the buildings date back to 1879.

CULTURAL GROUPS

Cowboy culture played an important role in Wyoming's history. Today, rodeos help to keep the tradition alive. Kaycee holds a rodeo called the Sheepherder's Rodeo. It features only sheep and sheepdogs. Old Trail Town in Cody is an outdoor museum displaying many historic buildings from across Wyoming. One of the buildings is the log cabin that outlaws Butch Cassidy and the Sundance Kid once used as a hideout.

Cowboy ballads are the folk music of Wyoming. Many of the original ballads came from the cowboys who took part in the cattle drives of the 1870s and 1880s. Today, traditional cowboy music is still sung on the range, and can be heard at county fairs and other state celebrations. Present-day country-and-western music can trace its musical roots back to cowboy ballads. Cowboy poetry contests and readings are another celebration of cowboy tradition.

QUICK FACTS

Lovell holds a rodeo called Mustang Days in June.

Women such as Mabel Strickland contributed to Wyoming's cowboy culture. Strickland was well known for her bronc riding. Other women became known for their roping stunts.

Each summer, the town of Sheridan has an annual cattle drive to celebrate its ranching heritage.

Many communities in Wyoming celebrate the state's ranching heritage with rodeos.

Wyoming's Native Peoples have a rich cultural heritage. Every year, they hold powwows to celebrate their history and traditions. The Shoshone and Arapaho hold powwows nearly every weekend during the summer on the Wind River Indian Reservation. Visitors to the powwows can also experience traditional Native-American arts, crafts, and foods.

The Arapaho Sun Dance takes place during the third week in July. During the festival, members of the Plains Native-American groups, such as the Cheyenne, the Arapaho, and the Shoshone, dance around a pole that is topped with a bison head. The bison is a symbol of plenty, and the dance is believed to bring good fortune for the following year.

Dancing competitions are some of the most popular events at the powwows held on the Wind River Indian Reservation.

Powwows were traditionally held before important events such as major hunts, marriage ceremonies, and other large gatherings.

QUICK FACTS

Cody calls itself the Rodeo Capital of the World and holds a rodeo every night during the summer.

As many as twelve different Native-American groups once lived in Wyoming, including the Cheyenne and the Sioux.

During the fourth week of June, the Shoshone celebrate the Shoshone Treaty Days and the Shoshone Indian Days and Rodeo.

The Wind River Reservation was the only reservation in the country where Native Americans were allowed to choose the land upon which they would live. It covers about 2 million acres of land.

Before his death in 1917, Buffalo Bill claimed to have killed over 4,000 bison.

ARTS AND ENTERTAINMENT

Buffalo Bill Cody was one of Wyoming's most well-known entertainers. Cody also played an important role in Wyoming history. Buffalo Bill, who was born William F. Cody, delivered mail on horseback for the **Pony Express**. Cody made the longest Pony Express ride ever. He later became a Union scout and soldier during the American Civil War. A talented marksman, Cody got his nickname by shooting buffalo and bringing the meat back to the men working on the transcontinental railroad.

In 1883, Buffalo Bill created the Wild West Show, which toured throughout North America and Europe. Highlights of the show included Native-American leader Sitting Bull and sharpshooter Annie Oakley. Oakley was able to shoot a playing card that was thrown in the air a dozen times before it hit the ground. As a result of his Wild West Show, Cody became a national celebrity.

QUICK FACTS

Buffalo Bill Cody founded the town of Cody. The town's Buffalo Bill Museum displays cowboy gear, firearms, and other artifacts from Buffalo Bill's life.

At the beginning of the twentieth century, nearly every town in Wyoming had its own opera house.

The Jackson Hole Fall Arts Festival is held every fall and gives artists the opportunity to show their work.

The first theater group in Wyoming came to Cheyenne in 1867. The troupe traveled by stagecoach. Today, visitors can take stagecoach tours of towns across the state.

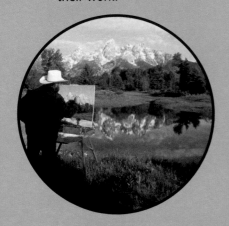

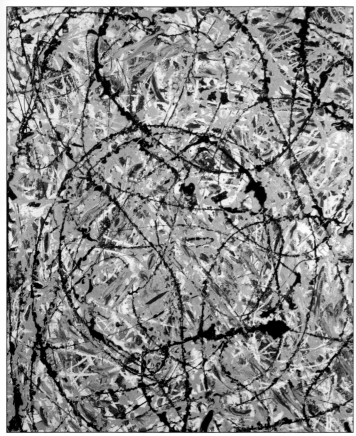

Watery Paths was created by Jackson Pollock using his drip-and-splatter style of painting.

Throughout its history, artists have tried to capture the beauty of Wyoming in paintings, drawings, and photographs. The National Museum of Wildlife Art, in Jackson Hole, contains more than 2,000 works of art, many of which were inspired by Wyoming.

Artist Jackson Pollock was born in Cody in 1912. Pollock was one of the first artists of the **abstract expressionist** movement. Pollock developed a form of painting where he dripped and splattered paint on a large canvas that was placed on the floor. Pollock never touched the picture with the brush. Sometimes, he even poured the paint straight out of the can. This form of painting is known as "action painting." It focuses on the process of painting rather than the finished product.

The University of Wyoming has many classical music groups, which include a symphony orchestra and a choir. The Grand Teton Music Festival, held annually at Teton Village in Jackson Hole, celebrates music through performances on indoor and outdoor stages.

The Grand Teton Music Festival attracts music lovers from across the country.

QUICK FACTS

Polka dancers from around the country come to Sheridan each year for the Bighorn Mountain Polka Days.

Actor Harrison Ford lives on a ranch that he built in Jackson Hole.

Isabel Jewell was a talented actor in the 1930s and 1940s. She played the role of Emmy Slattery in the blockbuster movie *Gone With the Wind*.

Every year on the fourth of July, Jackson Hole holds a free outdoor concert as part of the Grand Teton Music Festival. The concert attracts more than 10,000 people, which is more than the entire population of the town.

SPORTS

Jackson Hole is a popular destination for hang gliders. The nearby Rocky Mountains provide plenty of excellent launch sites.

Wyoming has no major-league sports teams, but amateur teams keep sports fans cheering. The University of Wyoming has both men's and women's basketball teams, a women's volleyball team, swimming and wrestling teams, and a rodeo club. Many other sports are popular with residents and visitors. *Volksmarches*, which translates as "people walks," are long hikes through the beautiful Wyoming scenery.

Both Yellowstone National Park and Grand Teton National Park provide many opportunities for outdoor recreation. Hiking and camping are popular in the forests and mountains of Yellowstone, while the more remote Grand Teton is an ideal location for backpacking, horseback riding, white-water rafting, fishing, and wildlife watching. Hunting is another popular sport in Wyoming. People may apply for licenses to hunt elk, deer, antelope, moose, bighorn sheep, and other animals.

QUICK FACTS

Sportscaster Curt Gowdy was born in Wyoming. He was the radio voice of the New York Yankees and the Boston Red Sox. In the 1960s, he switched from broadcasting baseball to football.

Wyoming is a popular fishing location. It has 15,846 miles of fishing streams and 297,633 acres of fishing lakes. A total of 3,400 lakes, ponds, and reservoirs are home to ninety types of fish.

Hot-air ballooning is popular in Wyoming. Riverton holds a Rendezvous Rally with thirty balloons each year, while Rock Springs holds the Annual Desert Balloon Extravaganza.

Wyoming has ten ski resorts. Skiing and snowmobiling are popular winter pursuits.

With its spectacular scenery, Wyoming is a perfect spot for hot-air ballooning. The morning is the best time for flights as the wind is calmer.

Rodeo events are considered some of the most dangerous sporting events in the world.

Wyoming is well known for its rodeo sports. Most rodeos feature five or more events. Popular events include saddle **bronc** riding, bareback bronc riding, bull riding, steer wrestling, and calf roping. In bull riding, contestants try to remain on a bucking bull for eight seconds. If the rider stays on for the full amount of time, judges rate the ride. In steer wrestling, or bulldogging, competitors must tackle a steer from their horse, grab it by the horns, and then toss it to the ground.

During calf and steer-roping contests, participants race against the clock to see how quickly and how well they can capture and tie up the animals. In the chuck-wagon races, contestants in horse-drawn wagons race around a track. Another popular rodeo sport is barrel racing. Competitors must race around a course of barrels on a horse, and the rider with the best time wins. Points are lost for any barrels that are knocked over.

QUICK FACTS

The Frontier Days Rodeo in Cheyenne is one of the oldest and biggest in the country.

Country musician Chris LeDoux won the world championship for bareback bronc riding in 1976. LeDoux grew up in Cheyenne.

In February, the International Pedigree Stage Stop Sled Dog Race winds through nine Wyoming counties. It takes competitors eleven days to complete the 500-mile course.

In barrel racing, riders must circle three barrels in a cloverleaf pattern. The barrels are arranged in a triangle.

Brain Teasers

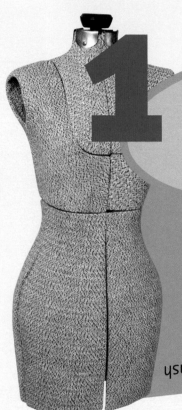

1

Which famous store got its start in Kemmerer?

Answer: JCPenney. James Cash Penney opened his first store in 1902. Today, JCPenney operates more than 1,140 stores across North America.

2

Robert Parker was the real name of which famous outlaw?

a. The Sundance Kid

b. Jesse James

c. Butch Cassidy

d. Billy the Kid

Answer: c. Butch Cassidy

3

Who invented the "dude ranch"?

Answer: The Eaton Ranch, near Wolf, was the first "dude ranch." A dude ranch is both a working ranch and a vacation spot for tourists from the city.

4

Where is the biggest coal mine in the United States?

Answer: The biggest coal mine in the United States is in Black Thunder. The mine is located in northeastern Wyoming near the town of Wright.

5 What is written on the city limits sign outside of Fort Laramie?

a. Welcome to the Big Fort!

b. 250 Good People and Six Sore Heads

c. City of the Bucking Bronco

d. Wyoming at its Best!

Answer: b. 250 Good People and Six Sore Heads.

6 What is the town of Afton known for?

Answer: Afton is home to the largest antler arch in the world. The arch stretches over a four-lane road.

7 Which horse is the model for the Bucking Horse and Rider trademark?

Answer: The horse is believed to be modeled after Steamboat, one of the best bucking horses of all-time. He was known as "the horse that couldn't be ridden."

8 Which well-known Wyoming landmark was featured in the movie *Close Encounters of the Third Kind*?

Answer: Devil's Tower, the huge formation of volcanic rock, is the site where a spaceship lands in the movie.

FOR MORE INFORMATION

Books

Evans, Lisa Gollin. *An Outdoor Family Guide to Yellowstone and Grand Teton National Parks*. Seattle: The Mountaineers Books: 1996.

Fradin, Dennis B. and Judith Bloom Fradin. *Wyoming.* From Sea to Shining Sea Series. Chicago: Children's Press, 1994.

Heinrichs, Ann. *America the Beautiful: Wyoming.* Chicago: Children's Press, 1992.

Web sites

You can also go online and have a look at the following Web sites:

State of Wyoming
http://www.state.wy.us/state/welcome.html

Wyoming Secretary of State
http://soswy.state.wy.us/informat/informat.htm

Stately Knowledge: Wyoming
http://www.ipl.org/youth/stateknow/wy1.html

Some Web sites stay current longer than others. To find other Wyoming Web sites, enter search terms such as "Yellowstone," "Cheyenne," "Buffalo Bill Cody," or any other topic you want to research.

GLOSSARY

abstract expressionist: a type of experimental art where artists paint expressions rather than objects

archeologists: scientists who study early peoples through artifacts and remains

bronc: a rodeo horse that tries to buck off a rider

cholera: an infectious disease

compulsory: required by law

drought: a long period of time when there is little or no rain

expedition: a journey made for exploration

hydroelectricity: energy created from moving water

mammoths: prehistoric fur-covered elephants

Mormons: members of the Church of Jesus Christ of Latter-day Saints

municipalities: cities, towns, or villages

Pony Express: an early system for transporting mail using horses and riders

population density: the average number of people per unit of area

precipitation: rain, snow, or hail that falls to the earth's surface

rendezvous: a meeting place

scrubland: land covered with low trees or shrubs

terrain: land

treaties: formal agreements between two governments

INDEX